THE LITTLEST
LIFE COACH

THE LITTLEST LIFE COACH
by David E. Beroth

The Littlest Life Coach
by David E. Beroth

Printed in the United States
of America

ISBN 978-0-615-84380-3

© 2013, First Assembly
of God Church,
Des Moines, IA

For information: Des Moines First Assembly, 2725 Merle Hay Rd, Des Moines, IA 50310
mailus@desmoinesfirst.org

des moines first assembly
www.desmoinesfirst.org

Dedication

With much gratitude I dedicate this to Kelli, our incredible daughter-in-law.

Thank you for being a wonderful mother to Lukis and Karli. Your tireless care and attention to their every need provides a nurturing environment for them to know the Love of God. Your playful spirit encourages them to know the Joy of the Lord, which will be their strength.

[27] She watches over the affairs of her household and does not eat the bread of idleness. [28] Her children arise and call her blessed; her husband also, and he praises her: Proverbs 31:27-28 (NIV)

Lukis, you are a gift from heaven. I pray you will stay true to the foundation of your childhood. You bring grandma and me joy beyond words. My prayer is that I can always model the right path in life.

Levi, you are a blessed man.

The godly walk with integrity; blessed are their children who follow them. Proverbs 20:7 (NLT)

Acknowledgements

I am so grateful for the privilege of serving the community of Christ followers at Des Moines First Assembly. Thank you for the idea of putting these lessons to paper. Thank you for loving my family! You motivate me to be the best I can be. I will always be indebted to the kindness of people like June Evans who ask about Lukis and Karli every Sunday.

I very much appreciate the assistance of Brittney Roorda. Your attention to the details helped make this project a reality. Thank you from the depth of my heart.

I am grateful for people like Janet Drake and Diana Koontz who proved to be essential. Thank you for your gift of time to read through these stories and offer helpful suggestions.

I will always be indebted to Paulette Langwith who helped refine these lessons. You held each story up to the light and examined it to grasp and more fully understand the core issue. Thank you for the gift of discovery.

Lori Nordstrom, thank you for the permission to use your photos of Lukis. (Lori photographed Lukis in 2008 for the Doodles event). ©nordstromphoto.com

Craig Tassin, thank you for your creativity and fantastic design to display these life moments with my grandson. You are the ultimate professional. I am very grateful. *www.levelbdesign.com*

Table of Contents

Introduction

I was the guy who thought grandparents were a bit over zealous about their grandkids. I heard statements like, "If I knew grandkids were this great, I would have had them first." I laughed then, but now I understand. It's a grandparent thing. Until you have experienced it for yourself, just laugh.

My friend and fellow grandparent, Jerry, shared with me a special day he had with his 5-year-old grandson.

Riley and I had spent the day together watching a cartoon movie in the morning and then went to the Cog Railway in Colorado Springs to take the train up Pikes Peak. I purchased box lunches to eat on the train, which of course included a prize in his. As we were climbing the mountain, I got a pair of binoculars from my pack and gave them to Riley to use on the ride. I told him he could take them home and keep them when the ride was over. I had also brought a large package of M&M's which were sparingly distributed a few at a time during the trip. At some point during the ride, Riley turned to me and said, "Grandpa, when I grow up, I want to be a Grandpa."

"If I knew grandkids were this great, I would have had them first."

So, you can see I'm not the only one who thinks being a grandpa is exceptional!

When our daughter-in-law was pregnant with our first grandchild, I was thrilled with thoughts about the fun phases of being a grandpa. Then, when my grandson, Lukis, was born and I held him for the first time, I was both proud of our son and daughter-in-law, but oddly overwhelmed with thoughts of the responsibilities that went along with my new family role.

My focus was on all the things I would have to teach this newest member of our family. Little did I realize that being a grandparent would be a learning experience for me. Not only is my grandson teaching me things I never knew, but things I used to know. He is also teaching me to become more aware of things I saw in the past but didn't really notice.

I hope this devotional will help you attune yourself with things you used to know and maybe even bring something new to mind.

WEEK

1

Finding Approval

I Can't Wait to See You!

The moment Lukis had his first visit to our home I started a routine I have continued to this day. When I know he is coming over, I drop everything I am doing and wait for him at the front door.

Even when he was a baby – I knew he didn't recognize me yet, but I didn't care. I would wait at the window. However, as he has grown older, he has learned to look for me now. When our eyes meet – he smiles knowing that "Papa" is waiting for him. I just love him so much that I can't wait to see him, to hold him, to just spend time with him.

I believe Jesus is the same way. I believe He loves us so much that He simply waits for us, whether we recognize Him or not. Even though we believe He wants the best for us, we begin to compromise in our thoughts, decisions, and actions. We spend so much time trying to live the life we want, be successful on our own, create our own rules, etc. Before you know it, we are exhausted. In fact – you may even feel that He's not there at all, simply because you haven't allowed your eyes to meet.

28 "Are you tired? Worn out? Burned out on religion? Come to me. Get away with me and you'll recover your life. I'll show you how to take a real rest. 29 Walk with me and work with me—watch how I do it. Learn the unforced rhythms of grace. I won't lay anything heavy or ill-fitting on

Whether you recognize Him or not – He is always there, and is always waiting for you.

10

you. [30] *Keep company with me and you'll learn to live freely and lightly."*
Matthew 11:28-30 (MSG)

As Christ followers, we want so desperately to hear from God, but I have realized it means even more for us to take the time to see Him, too. I want to be clear – just because you don't see Him does not mean He's not there. He is absolutely present – it's just up to you to recognize Him. Start with simple things. Be grateful for what God has given you – your family – your home – your work – your car – the list goes on. You truly have an opportunity to see God every day with a smile, your time, your giving, or even in a simple word of encouragement that you share with someone else. Whether you recognize Him or not – He is always there, and is always waiting for you. In fact, He can't wait to see you!

What things in your life have kept you from seeing Him?

_____

_____

_____

_____

CLOSING THOUGHT

Lord – teach me to daily see you in my life. When my life becomes too busy and I rely on me – stir my heart to look for you.

God Is Thinking About You...

I love celebrating birthdays with Lukis. It was his 5th birthday and I picked Lukis up from school. We headed off to hit golf balls, practice putting, and look at new golf clubs. The Golfsmith store is the perfect place for Lukis and me to spend some one-on-one time.

After singing happy birthday to him I said, "Lukis, I am so glad God made you and allowed you to be born into our family! You are a wonderful blessing!" Like most five year olds, he started asking questions. Did God make the grass? Did God make cars? Did God make Karli (his 3-year-old sister)?

He has never stopped thinking about you.

I did my best answering his questions and it seemed to satisfy his curiosity until he asked the most inquisitive question of the day: "Papa, where was I before God made me?" Almost immediately I thought of Psalm 139 and said, "You were in God's thoughts — held in his love and his plan for your life." Lukis simply said, "Cool!"

As Lukis was focused on hitting golf balls, I was captivated by a God that lovingly thinks of us and plans our lives.

[13] You made all the delicate, inner parts of my body and knit me together in my mother's womb. [14] Thank you for making me so wonderfully

complex! Your workmanship is marvelous—how well I know it. ¹⁵ You watched me as I was being formed in utter seclusion, as I was woven together in the dark of the womb. ¹⁶ You saw me before I was born. Every day of my life was recorded in your book. Every moment was laid out before a single day had passed. ¹⁷ How precious are your thoughts about me, O God. They cannot be numbered! Psalm 139:13-17 (NLT)

As this special time together ended for Lukis and me, I was overwhelmed as I realized that God not only thought of Lukis, but every day of his life was prerecorded before he was even born. He thought of Lukis, He thought of me, and He absolutely thought of you.

The truth is – our lives can feel like the farthest thing from what God planned for us. However, that is the beauty of God – He has never stopped thinking about you. All you need to do is simply talk to Him. Ask Him to remind you of what He wants for your life. What did He have in mind when He created you? What does He desire for your life?

Take some time to reflect on what your heart is telling you, and remind yourself just how special you are to Him.

_____

_____

_____

_____

CLOSING THOUGHT

God – I pray that you send me daily reminders of how much you love me and in every life choice I make – remind my heart what you have planned for my life.

Holding Hands...

It is always a wonderful feeling when Lukis and I are walking together and he reaches up and grabs my hand. I don't always know what he is thinking, but my heart tells me this is where he feels safe and he knows I will make sure nothing will happen to him.

I never take those moments for granted and it makes my heart smile. I often wonder if that is what David felt in Psalm 139 when he said, "even there your hand will guide me, your right hand will hold me fast."

David had confidence in God's ability to guide him along the path God had chosen for him, just as Lukis has confidence in my ability to keep him safe. I have also wondered why David specified God's right hand. Does David simply have a vivid picture in mind of God reaching down with his strong hand, his coordinated hand, to guide and protect him? Or is there more to it?

Jesus grabbed our hand and put it into God's hand.

I don't know if David completely realized the full effect when he wrote these words, but I do know that God wanted so desperately to reach down to you and me that He sent His son. Jesus was and is God's love reaching down to us. Jesus grabbed our hand and put it into God's hand. He is the reaching right hand of God.

David's writings are not about religion or doctrine, but about relationship. When you have a relationship with Jesus, you want to grab the right hand of God – simply because He loves you and you trust in His ability to guide you in His plan for your life.

There are times you may feel completely alone, but I challenge you to simply reach up and grab His hand. He wants to love you, to guide you, and to keep you safe. Maybe your excitement on this journey has faded — you have lost hope, your sense of purpose, or even your joy. You may have even intentionally stopped pursuing God's plan and desires for your life, and you miss Him. Don't give up! Remember these three truths!

Truth #1: God has placed more within you than you realize.
Truth #2: You likely have settled for the life you have now.
Truth #3: God is still reaching out to you with His hand.

Reflect on what truths God has given you – are you willing to reach out and grab His hand?

_____

_____

_____

_____

CLOSING THOUGHT

God – today I reach up to grab your hand. Remind me of the desire I have to follow your plan for my life, knowing you will always be there to guide me if I just hold your hand.

Watch Me!

The week Lukis was born I purchased his first set of golf clubs (bag and all). He is now 6 and has been swinging a golf club from the time he could walk. We started in the house with plastic clubs and then graduated to the front lawn.

By the time he was three, I promoted him to the big leagues – the driving range. After a few instructions and practice swings, Lukis put his tee in the ground, placed the ball on the tee, took his perfect stance (compliments of Grandpa) and said, "Papa, watch me!" He said it every time he went to swing! There was no need for him to even ask. My eyes were glued on him.

I was enjoying our time at the driving range, and I began to reflect on God's attentive Spirit. Getting God's attention is easier than you think. My mind immediately raced to the story in the Old Testament where Gideon, by all accounts, was hiding and did not want any attention. Yet God's eyes were glued on him. He was preparing him for success. God identified him as a mighty warrior and confirmed for him that he would be strong and have power. God even told him, "I will be with you."

God actually showed up fifteen times, just to encourage Gideon in his faith to do one job. Now that's a personal God! It makes me wonder

My eyes were glued on him.

how many incredible things God has to do before I take the time to worship and praise Him for His patience, timing, reassurance, control, goodness, love, and more.

Here's the amazing part — don't miss this! In Judges 7:17 (NIV) Gideon said, "Watch me," he told them. "Follow my lead. When I get to the edge of the camp, do exactly as I do."

How did Gideon transition from hiding out in fear to commanding, "Watch me!"? He knew God was there for him – he knew that God was a personal God – and then he realized that God was always watching him.

Does your faith have you hiding from God? Are there things that are preventing you from understanding that He is a personal God?

_____

_____

_____

_____

CLOSING THOUGHT

Lord – today I pray that you become personal to me. Help me to realize that you are always there, always watching, and always encouraging my faith in you. When I start to hide – remind me I have the strength and power to accomplish what you have asked me to do.

You Smile, I Smile...

There is just something about Lukis that is contagious. When he is happy, you can't help but join him in being happy. No matter what the event – big or small – you simply want to celebrate with him.

One day, Lukis was telling me about an incredible day he had at school. It was one of those days that he believed nothing could go wrong. I said to Lukis with equal excitement, "I bet you made your teacher happy today!" He replied nonchalantly, "I make her smile a lot." I thought to myself what a wonderful perspective. Lukis knew he had "done good" when he made his teacher smile.

I began to think about what makes God smile. Is it my prayer time with Him? Is it the moments I choose to trust instead of worry? Is it kind words I use with my wife? I wonder how our lives would change if we simply made decisions that would make God smile.

May all my thoughts be pleasing to Him, for I rejoice in the Lord.
Psalms 104:34 (NLT)

The problem is there are so many temptations to make the people around us smile rather than God. It can be your parents, your children, your employer, or even your pastor. Without realizing it we often

Make Him big in your life.

focus our behaviors toward receiving the approving smile, nod or hug from someone in our life. Unfortunately, we also end up reacting to a disappointing frown and focus our time and energy on bringing back the smile we so desperately need to function. In the meantime, we miss out on God's smile. There is nothing wrong with making people happy, but when it becomes your focus – you not only lose out on His smile, you lose out on His purpose for your life.

The hardest thing about making the decision to please God is that those same people you worked so hard to please will not be happy with your change. After all, you are no longer focusing on them.

Know this: The desire to please people will only go away when we replace it with a greater love. In other words, the moment you shift your focus from people to God – and make Him big in your life – you will realize quickly that the approval of one (Him) is much greater than any other smile in your life.

What is distracting you from God's smile? Are there people in your life that you seek to please?

_____

_____

_____

_____

CLOSING THOUGHT

Lord – forgive me for losing sight of you – your smile. I pray that you surround me with the people that will help me to keep you as my focus. Give me the strength to make you big in my life and trust you even bigger!

Weekend Reflection

WEEK 1

What are my takeaways from this week?

_____

_____

What's true about me?

_____

_____

What do I want to be true about me?

_____

_____

How do I want to show up on Monday?

_____

_____

What needs to happen this weekend in order for this to be a reality?

_____

_____

WEEK 2

Making Room

Room for "Two"

Lukis had spent the entire day with us the day his baby sister (Karli) was born. His mom was obviously preoccupied in labor, so it was our privilege to help out. Elli and I did our best to entertain him as we all waited in anticipation.

We talked about his baby sister that would be here any minute. His mom and dad had prepared him well for this exciting arrival. Lukis would even sing "Jesus Loves Me" to Karli while she was in his mommy's tummy.

Finally at 2:30 p.m., Karli was born. A few hours later, we arrived at the hospital so Lukis could meet his baby sister for the first time. Lukis had obviously enjoyed front and center attention from everyone for almost two years, but when we entered that room, it didn't take long to realize someone else had stepped into his spotlight. I don't think he had calculated the cost (and sacrifice) of having a baby sister.

Lukis discovered that love was much bigger than he realized.

He looked at Karli politely but didn't want Elli or me paying too much attention to that wrapped up bundle. When any of the grandparents would take their turn holding her, Lukis would act out, as if to say, "I will not stand for my prominent place in this family as first grandchild to be diminished by this new invasion."

The day of Karli's birth was also the day Lukis discovered that love was much bigger than he realized. At a minimum – there was definitely room for two. Watching Lukis accept Karli into his world has been a refresher course in Relationships 101. For two years Lukis enjoyed the focus, deep devotion, affection, and consistency of our unconditional love for him, without interruption. We played with him by the hour and gave him wonderful gifts. We encouraged him, sang to him, listened to him, and believed in him. It's hard to imagine that this same love could be given to anyone, but that's how God works.

God loves you with all His heart and devotion. He loves you so much that He gave His one and only Son to die on a cross so you could live with Him forever in heaven. There is no greater love. Jesus said,

"'Love the Lord your God with all your passion and prayer and intelligence.' This is the most important, the first on any list. But there is a second to set alongside it: 'Love others as well as you love yourself.'" Matthew 22:37-39 (MSG)

Take a few moments to reflect on just how much God loves you – unconditionally. Is that kind of love difficult for you to understand? Why?

_____

_____

_____

_____

CLOSING THOUGHT

God – thank you for loving me – not because of what I do, but just because I belong to you. Teach me to love others in a way that reflects you in my life. And if I don't tell you enough – I pray that today you see my heart and how full of love it is for you – my creator.

The "Un"Happy Meal

Lukis has a beautiful baby sister named Karli. It was an easy decision to make time to celebrate her first birthday with her which, of course, included my favorite life coach, Lukis. We decided to eat at one of their favorite (fun) restaurants.

God empowers you to be a peacemaker, not a troublemaker.

While I was bringing our tray of food over to the table, I overheard Lukis telling Elli that a little boy hit him while they were in the play area. I could see that Lukis was quite troubled about this. He let it go enough to start eating, but about the time his chicken nuggets were gone, he asked me, "Papa, why did that boy hit me?"

Without wanting to find that little boy myself, I did try to explain why some people are rude, selfish or just plain mean. Even though he is very bright, I observed he was still bothered by the fact that another boy would hit him for no reason. So, I changed the focus and helped him understand what his response should be if that might happen again. The truth is, God wants us to live in peace (and joy) with everyone. In fact, God empowers you to be a peacemaker, not a troublemaker.

You can develop a healthy, robust community that lives right with God and enjoy its rewards only if you do the hard work of getting along with each other, treating each other with dignity and honor. James 3:18 (MSG)

It is no secret that the stresses of our lives can often prevent us from "rising above" the situation. Obviously with Lukis there was a protective moment in me, but I knew it was much more important to teach him how to respond in this unhappy moment. As adults, the issues of life can hurt much more than a quick hit in the play area. In fact, I would not want to minimize any hurt you may feel, so let me offer a few thoughts to you:

- Attack the problem, not the person. Protect the relationship, but speak the truth in love.
- Cooperate whenever possible. Let go of hurt and anger.
- Actively focus on promoting reconciliation, not resolution. Reconciliation ends hostility, but it doesn't mean you've resolved all the issues.

I know this is so much easier said than done, but I encourage you to start somewhere, even if it's just a simple prayer.

Is there an opportunity for you to be a peacemaker in your life?

_____

_____

_____

_____

CLOSING THOUGHT

Lord — help me to understand that you empower me to live in peace. Teach me to let go of things that have caused stress and distraction and direct me to the peace you intended me to have.

Juggling Our Joy

Lukis is fascinated with any type of ball. Every time he visits our church he wants to see all the sports memorabilia in my office. One Sunday I did a sermon illustration that used a baseball, basketball, football, and golf ball.

Between services, I brought Lukis to my office and he was thrilled to see all the different types of balls. It didn't take long for this little one to become completely overwhelmed, as he tried to play with all of them at the same time. He would pick up the football and then try to pick up the basketball, only to drop the football. Having the basketball in hand, his attention would drift to the baseball, only to drop the basketball. At one time, he successfully had the baseball and golf ball in each hand, only to ponder how he could pick up the football. I watched to see how he would remedy this dilemma. Finally after exhaustion set in, Lukis brought each ball to me one by one. He then would take one and play with it for a while, then give it back and take another in its place. That was when he started having fun.

As humorous as this exchange was to watch, I realized as an adult we can try to hold onto too much. In doing so we never take full grasp of any one thing. We become fearful, thinking at any moment something will slip right through our fingers, never realizing that with our own choices we are limiting both our joy and our peace of mind.

There will always be something new that we try to hold on to.

26

I have often felt the frustration my grandson experienced that day in my office – so much to do and so many opportunities. I always want to do it all. But my age and experience have given me a small advantage over my grandson, to reflect where my life is and where it needs to be in the years to come.

On the one hand, I have seen so many considerable things happen in and through my life. Yet on the other hand, I have experienced times when I've fallen short, grieved God, and not been the quality person I desired to be. What made the difference? When I got it right, I loosened my grip and focused on that one thing God placed before me. In those moments, I was not consumed with anxiety nor was I trying to be everything, do everything or have everything. Those times were seasons of clear perspective and cloudless priorities.

I would love to say I have learned and I always choose right – but that's the difficulty of our human nature. There will always be something new that we try to hold on to, only to realize our hands aren't big enough. However, God's hands are wonderful. Hand your desires, wants and needs to Him and pray about the things you should give focus to. You will no longer need to juggle your joy – it will just be there.

Are there things in your life that are causing you to juggle? What is God asking you to release to Him?

_____

_____

_____

_____

CLOSING THOUGHT

God — I give these "things" to you. Teach me to focus on what pleases you and where you need me to be. I release any thing that is limiting the joy you have planned for me.

Grandma's Money

For Easter one year, my wife, Elli, sent Lukis an Easter card. Lukis, of course, opened it with great excitement, but was puzzled when he discovered a dollar bill in the card.

He looked up at his mom and said, "This is Grandma's money. I will give it back to her." Kelli explained that the dollar was Grandma's, but she sent it to him as a gift and even better, he could keep it.

Lukis thought this dollar bill was an extravagant gift. He didn't know that Grandma has a few more dollar bills hidden in her purse. However, Lukis' experience with this dollar bill reminded me of a truth to live by – a truth that is most often overlooked. A steward, by proper definition, cannot be an owner. A steward is a caretaker, one who manages things that belong to someone else. This definition is best illustrated by the Psalmist David's thought,

"The earth is the Lord's, and everything in it. The world and all its people belong to him." Psalms 24:1 (NLT)

As adults we understand that this dollar bill was a gift to Lukis, but what if we applied his thought process to every financial decision we made? What if we truly understood that everything we have belongs to the Lord? Would we make different decisions? Would we take better care

Everything we have belongs to the Lord

of our stuff? More importantly, would we be able to give a good report back to God that we took excellent care of what He had given us?

Challenge yourself to include the Lord in every decision you make, understanding that nothing we have belongs to us.

Do you have a true understanding of stewardship? Do you need to renew your understanding that everything belongs to Him?

_____

_____

_____

_____

CLOSING THOUGHT

Lord — forgive me for losing sight that I am a manager of everything you have given me. Challenge me to make every decision with you in mind.

Deep Pockets

Lukis came to me with his piggy bank and without hesitation, I reached into my pants pocket and pulled out several coins. I gave them to him one by one and watched his tiny fingers carefully drop each one into the special slot.

When I thought the piggy bank had been amply fed, I went on to other things and then sat on the couch in our living room. I soon realized Lukis was not only staring at my other pocket, but a little hand had started its way in search of a few more coins. His subtle movement was asking, "Is there more, Grandpa?"

I asked Lukis, "Do you need some more coins? Go ahead and get some." He tried but the pockets were too deep. So he said, "You get 'em Papa, I can't reach 'em." I did, of course, and the purposeful routine repeated itself as he placed the additional coins in his bank. I thought, "I wish I could trust God enough to live that way – to know that He has what I am looking for – to simply reach my hand into God's pocket – to have my eyes on everything He wants to give me – to reach out for everything He has planned just for me." The truth is – it may be out of my reach, but it is never out of His.

It may be out of my reach, but it is never out of His.

⁴ But because of his great love for us, God, who is rich in mercy, ⁵ made us alive with Christ even when we were dead in transgressions — it is by grace you have been saved. ⁶ *And God raised us up with Christ and seated us with him in the heavenly realms in Christ Jesus,* ⁷ *in order that in the coming ages he might show the incomparable riches of his grace, expressed in his kindness to us in Christ Jesus.* Ephesians 2:4-7 (NIV)

We don't really understand all the ways of God. Yet, His desire is to pour an incredible, never ending amount of grace into our lives. You will never realize everything that God has for you, until you reach into His pockets. After all, He has everything you need.

What prevents you from trusting that God has everything you need?

CLOSING THOUGHT

Lord — today I pray for faith in you. I spend a lot of time and effort trying to figure things out on my own and often forget that you have everything I need. Lord, remind me that no matter what, my needs are never out of your reach.

Weekend Reflection

WEEK 2

What are my takeaways from this week?

_____

_____

What's true about me?

_____

_____

What do I want to be true about me?

_____

_____

How do I want to show up on Monday?

_____

_____

What needs to happen this weekend in order for this to be a reality?

_____

_____

WEEK

3

Being Authentic

Make-Believe

It was my grandson's first trip to California. Lukis loved being chased by the waves and building sand castles for two days, only to be topped by an entire day spent at Disneyland.

Disney did not disappoint, as the Magic Kingdom was filled with Disney characters and any ride Lukis could get Grandma to attempt. Lukis was even chosen to be trained as a Jedi to fight Darth Vader. Needless to say, these were three big days in the life of a 5-year-old boy.

While packing to go home, Grandma Elli said to Lukis, "Tomorrow we have to go back to our real lives." Lukis replied, "Grandma, I like our fake life!"

You will have to be honest about the choices you have made.

Each of us has probably felt like Lukis at one time or another. The life we intended to live or have made up in our head is so much more glamorous than the life we are actually living. We want so badly to have a different life that we begin to live for tomorrow. In just two more years, or six years, or 10 years, I will finally be able to make a change. You may not know what that change is right now, but we can absolutely make believe it is so much better than today.

There is nothing wrong with wanting a better life or situation, but if it involves avoiding life today or drifting from one escape to another, it is time to do a reality check. That reality check begins with a heart-to-

heart conversation with God. It is highly likely that the life you have today is a result of a series of choices you have made. No matter how hopeless your situation may seem, remember this thought – you did not get here overnight, but God can absolutely show you the way out.

The hardest question to ask is this: "Are you willing to make changes?" Again, no matter your situation, for you to truly do and become something different – change will be required. There is one catch: You will have to be honest about the choices you have made. Acknowledge where you are today.

Examine yourselves to see if your faith is genuine. Test yourselves.
2 Corinthians 13:5 (NLT)

Do you have the faith to take the risk and make that change? Are there old habits you need to break? Are there new habits you need to start? Be encouraged by starting one thing at a time, and allow your "new life" to become the journey God intended. There will be speed bumps and moments you feel discouraged, but God wants nothing more than for you to live the life He intended you to have.

What aspects of your life cause you to daydream or want something more?

_____

_____

_____

_____

CLOSING THOUGHT

God – I commit my life to you. I pray that you guide me one step at a time to stop wishing for something more and realize you have always intended for me to prosper in my work, in my finances, and in my family. Lord – teach me each day that every decision I make can take me one step closer to the life you intended me to live.

I'm Bored!

With dreary faces, Lukis and Karli announced the two most irksome words known to a mom, "I'm bored!" I appreciate Kelli, our daughter-in-law. She is very resourceful, but in that moment she was thinking "Oh no!

It's already starting and they're only 5 and 3!" However, instead of becoming frustrated, she turned to the next best thing – Pinterest. And this is what she found: An "I'm Bored" jar!

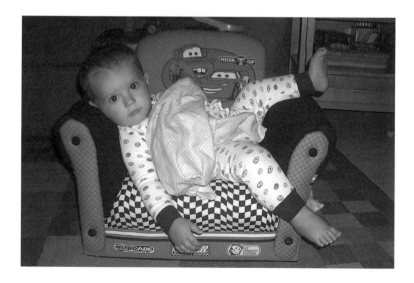

The jar is filled with tongue depressor sticks with chores, tasks, and fun things to do. For the rest of the summer, every time Lukis or Karli announced, "I'm bored!" they would reach into that jar and do what the stick said. It was such a success, Kelli figured out quickly that "I'm bored!" really meant, I want to see what's in the jar today!

Many people, including Christians, are utterly bored with life. Boredom is a combination of weariness, listlessness, and unconcern that causes a person to feel like doing nothing. I'm bored just thinking about it. We have even disguised boredom in our responses. For example, the term "whatever" is used as a response to politely say, "I don't even care enough to give you an answer." When you are bored, there is nothing to do because there is nothing that matters.

Boredom — it's not a God thing — it's a focus thing.

Isn't that how we often approach our walk with Christ? Many people only attend church if there is a "show" because they have a need to be entertained. Don't get me wrong, I love an illustrated sermon, but if your attendance is dependent on that method – you may be bored. Or perhaps you absolutely know that God has a calling on your life, but it would require too much from you right now, so you simply respond, "whatever." If God really wants it to happen – He will make it happen.

I often wonder what would happen if God had an "I'm Bored" jar. Would you be as excited as Lukis and Karli to see what great things God has in store for you? You have to realize this one thing when it comes to boredom – it's not a God thing – it's a focus thing. What are you focusing on? If you're bored – the focus will always be on you. Let me challenge you: If God has placed a calling on your life – you are the only one who can fill it.

For God's gift and His call can never be withdrawn.
Romans 11:29 (NLT)

And if you need a little excitement in your Sunday service – show up! Let God do the rest. You might be surprised at how amazing the Spirit of God can be.

Are you finding yourself bored? What areas of life feel mundane?

_____

_____

_____

_____

CLOSING THOUGHT

God – I want to be excited about you. Teach me that when I'm bored, I am only focusing on me. Challenge me to reach into your "I'm Bored" jar and do the things that need to be done!

Above The Line...

Lukis could not contain his excitement when he yelled, "Papa, I earned 17 frogs today! I broke the record!" Don't worry — our family will not be making a guest appearance on *Swamp People* any time soon.

Evaluate the desires of your heart.

Lukis earned 17 frogs for "above the line" behavior at school. His kindergarten teacher uses the "Above the Line" behavior management approach with her students. Above and below are concepts most children grasp at a young age. Thus she rewards them with a frog when behaviors are above the line, and encourages them to self-correct when they fall short. My Lukis broke the record. In fact, I would not be a true grandpa if I didn't also tell you he has never been below the line.

As proud as I was of Lukis, I wondered if I took advantage of every opportunity to be "above the line" in my Christian walk. I'm not talking about performance or bartering with the Lord. I'm talking about the simple definition of Christianity – to be Christ like – a follower of Christ. The struggle we have is free will. We get so focused on sin (below the line) that we forget it is our desires that give birth to sin.

[14] *Temptation comes from our own desires, which entice us and drag us away.* [15] *These desires give birth to sinful actions. And when sin is allowed to grow, it gives birth to death. James 1:14-15 (NLT)*

If you struggle with sin in your life (and sometimes, a repeatable sin), let me challenge you to evaluate the desires of your heart. Keeping our desires in check will give us the opportunity to self-correct. Many of us have been disappointed in God because He has promised to grant the desires of our heart, yet nothing has come to pass. Do you truly know what your heart desires? Is it to be closer to God? To reach the lost? To feed the hungry? Or is it to have a bigger home? A nicer car? To golf under par? I do believe that God can bless you with many things (including material things), but it can never replace your desire for Him.

If you find your Christian walk falling "below the line" and you are tired of the daily struggle, it may be time to simply review your desires – all of them. Spend some time with the Lord and do a little housekeeping. You may be surprised at what you find!

Are there things you desire that have the potential to birth sin? Are there desires that need to be put in check?

_____

_____

_____

_____

CLOSING THOUGHT

Lord – I am tired of the struggle and know you truly want to bless me. Teach me to desire you first.

Make Good Choices!

One morning at the breakfast table, my son and daughter-in-law were reviewing a Sunday school lesson with Lukis. The lesson focused on making choices that please God.

It was particularly good timing for Lukis, as he was not responding well to changes in his world now that Karli, his sister, had arrived. Plus, to make matters worse, his mom had added another child to her daily routine to earn additional income. Clearly, Lukis was going to be challenged and would need to acquire some new coping skills.

Within a day, it was clear that Lukis had exhausted his sharing skills with his new friend and lost patience with his baby sister, who was chewing on his puzzle pieces. He found himself sitting in the corner waiting for his sentence in time-out to be complete. Just before the timer went off, he called for his mom and, with all heartfelt sincerity, said, "Mom, I'm ready to make good choices."

I have often thought that as adults we need a good time-out, especially if the result is better choices. Life is a process of choices. In our early years (like Lukis), our life is determined mainly by our conditions. Lukis did not choose his family or where to live – he certainly did not choose a baby sister. His choices are in response to others' choosing – his parents' choices. But as his age increases, so will his options.

You can choose your actions or you can choose your consequences, but you can't choose both.

As our choices increase, we are confronted with the reality that our today is predominantly a reflection and result of the choices we made yesterday. Our decisions determine our destinies. The sooner we make the right choices, the better off we are today.

Think about this principle: You can choose your actions or you can choose your consequences, but you can't choose both. For every action, there is a consequence or a reward. When you are caught in a result of bad choices – it can be difficult to turn things around. However, that's where God comes in – give yourself a time-out with Him, and determine within yourself to make better choices.

[16] *Make the most of every opportunity for doing good in these evil days.* [17] *Don't act thoughtlessly, but try to understand what the Lord wants you to do.* Ephesians 5:16-17 (NLT)

Are there choices in your life that need to change? Are you willing to give yourself a time-out with God?

_____

_____

_____

_____

CLOSING THOUGHT

God — let my daily choices be with you in mind. Teach me to make good choices — to pray over the choices I do make and take the time-out with you so that I can understand what you want me to do.

Get Naked!

I've never seen anyone enjoy a bath as much as my Lukis. The minute his body touches the water, he smiles and has a look of complete relaxation, as if he is sitting in a Jacuzzi. Maybe it's the combination of the bubbles and toys.

Or maybe he is preparing for his "little ritual" after the bath. When Lukis spends the night at our home, as soon as he finishes his bath, he finds a way to scoot out of the bathroom and runs around the living room shouting, "Naked boy! Naked boy! Try and catch the naked boy!" After a while of chasing him I will catch him in a big towel and help him with his pajamas. We then wind down for the evening with a book or one of his favorite kid shows.

I love my grandson's passion for making the most of bath time. He adds joy and laughter to what could be a painstaking task for some youngsters and parents. "Naked boy," as Lukis describes himself, is a true picture of authenticity and vulnerability.

God wants me to be naked and not ashamed. He wants me to run towards people and relationships with authenticity and vulnerability.

Now, although Adam and his wife were both naked, neither of them felt any shame. Genesis 2:25 (NLT)

Sadly, what I tend to do is cover up from God and run the other direction. Why do I do this? Because the story of Adam and Eve is my story, too. Like them, I started out my relationship with God willing to be naked and unashamed, until I fell into a messy world because of sin – my sin. Rather than risk feeling disappointed, I refuse to be vulnerable and lose my authenticity. I cover up.

That is not a place to enjoy God's intended life for me. God wanted me to have a transparent heart – yes, even to be vulnerable at times. It is when I am transparent that people not only see what is in my heart, they also see the God I serve.

To develop your relationship with God and find an incredible passion for Him, you have to be willing to become vulnerable – naked and not ashamed. Let down your guard, be transparent, and show your heart. In other words, Get Naked!

What is keeping you "covered up"? What will it take for you to be naked before Him?

Be willing to become vulnerable – naked and not ashamed.

CLOSING THOUGHT

Lord — teach me to be vulnerable with you. No matter what I have experienced in life, I know you can use it for my good — but it requires that I be transparent. Let others see you in me, even in my mess.

Weekend Reflection

What are my takeaways from this week?

_____

_____

What's true about me?

_____

_____

What do I want to be true about me?

_____

_____

How do I want to show up on Monday?

_____

_____

What needs to happen this weekend in order for this to be a reality?

_____

_____

WEEK
4

Feeling Stronger

Caller ID

After I finished a meeting, I reached into my briefcase to grab my phone and noticed I had a missed call from my daughter-in-law. She did not leave a message.

I decided to try to call her on my way home and her phone went straight to voice mail. As I walked into the house I saw Elli was on the phone – and it was Lukis. Apparently, he had tried to call me earlier (with his mom's phone) and was telling Grandma how frustrated he was that Papa did not answer his call. I believe his exact words were, "Why won't my Papa answer his phone?"

I completely understand. I do not like busy signals, unanswered calls or even voice mail. I would like for you to pick up if you see me calling. Is that too much to ask? Lukis didn't think so! Even the Psalmist could relate:

We don't have to face those frustrations or disappointments alone.

Don't turn away from me in my time of distress. Bend down to listen, and answer me quickly when I call to you. Psalm 102:2 (NLT)

Have you ever felt that way? Have you been frustrated with delays, slow responses, and interruptions, and just when you think you are moving forward – discouragement starts to seep in? We sometimes find ourselves challenged by those situations and, if I'm honest – just plain disappointed.

The wonderful news is we don't have to face those frustrations or disappointments alone. God is always there. We simply have to call out to Him. He always answers.

The LORD has heard my plea; the LORD will answer my prayer.
Psalm 6:9 (NLT)

Lukis called me again, and I made a point to answer his call. I heard his excitement as he yelled out to his mom, "Papa answered!" Lukis just wanted to sing me a new song he had learned, and then asked if he could bring over his new DVD's. He continued to shout with excitement at my every response. Our phone conversation was such a wonderful reminder of the relationship we have with Christ. Whether we want to talk to Him about a frustration or a blessing, He will always pick up. He knows it's you.

What frustrations have kept you from calling the Lord? Are you fearful that He won't answer?

_____

_____

_____

_____

CLOSING THOUGHT

Lord — remind me that nothing is off limits for you. I don't have to do this life alone and if I just call out to you, you will answer — every time. Lord, give me the courage to simply reach out to you first.

I Don't Want to Die!

We have all been confused at one point or another about God, about heaven, and about faith.

When Lukis was 3, he asked his mom an incredible question, "Mommy – what is heaven?" Kelli quickly explained, "It's a place that God made for people who believe in Him, and they go there when they die." Lukis took a moment and responded, "I don't believe in God."

It's hard to imagine a 3-year-old mind trying to comprehend heaven, much less God – but adding death to boot? I'm positive his mind was screaming, "I don't want to die." Kelli did not let him dwell in the gloom and doom – but began to fill his mind with all of the Bible stories he loved like Daniel and the lion's den, and David and Goliath. Kelli even talked about a Sunday school lesson, explaining that if you believe in Jesus, you believe in God. After all, Jesus is God's son. Lukis knows his Bible stories, and he quickly informed his mother that Jesus was the son of Mary and Joseph.

After many reiterations of God, Jesus, heaven and life, Lukis declared that night that he once again believed in God. The amazing thing is we have all been confused at one point or another about God, about heaven, and about faith. This confusion may have happened as a result of an unanswered prayer or a trial that has drained you spiritually, emotionally, and physically. In that moment you may have said, "I don't believe in God" – or something close to those words. You may have asked, if there is a God, why would this happen to me? Why do good people have to die?

I want you to know that it is absolutely okay to be confused about God or things that happen in your life. However, in those moments when you don't know what or how to pray – talk to Him. Tell Him what you are feeling. If you need more faith – ask Him. If you need strength – ask Him. If you need answers – read His Word, go to church, and surround yourself with godly men and women. Kelli spent an entire day reassuring Lukis about God's goodness. God knew we would need each other to encourage and lift each other up, or simply remind each other to trust in Him!

Do not let your hearts be troubled. Trust in God; trust also in me.
John 14:1 (NIV)

Are there areas in your life that challenge your belief in God?

_____

_____

_____

_____

CLOSING THOUGHT

Lord – in the moments I lose sight of you, I pray that you allow me to see you in such an incredible way. Teach me daily to trust in you, and when my heart feels troubled, remind me that you are there!

Ducks and Geese and Wind — Oh My!

Lukis and I were sitting on our porch looking at Grandma Elli's duck figures. Of course, Lukis' curiosity took over and the conversation quickly shifted to the difference between wooden ducks, real ducks and geese that swim in the pond.

The truth is this power is available to each of us.

Suddenly without warning, a gust of wind blew so hard that the trees were bent and the siding on our house began to clatter – it even startled me! With his eyes as big as saucers, Lukis asked, "Papa! What was that?!"

I didn't know how to answer except with the obvious, "It was the wind, Lukis." However, it was such an unexpected wind, I couldn't help but reflect the couple of verses in Acts 2. It was the day of Pentecost, and all the disciples were together in the upper room. "Suddenly," the Bible says, "there was a noise from heaven like the sound of a mighty wind!" There was significance with the wind. Jesus had told them that "you will receive power" and what better way to describe power than with a sudden, unexpected wind.

The truth is this power is available to each of us. It was a promise from Jesus himself that God would send someone in His place. Many of us need this power in our lives, but we would rather try to control the situation ourselves than risk allowing this power to take over. This power, which is the Holy Spirit, is simply something most people do not understand.

In fact, we have heard so many conflicting theologies about the Holy Spirit that we are simply confused. However, rather than add one more "opinion" to the mix, I want to encourage you to understand that the Holy Spirit is a "gift" from God himself. Read the book of Acts and ask God to open your heart and mind to what the Holy Spirit (this power) is intended to be in your life.

If there is one ongoing theme throughout this devotional, it is to challenge YOU to have a personal relationship with Christ. I'm not just talking about giving your heart to the Lord; I'm talking about giving your life to him with a sincere willingness to embark on a daily journey with Christ — a willingness to open your eyes in a way that feels vulnerable, yet teachable – a way that accepts His power in your life.

What is preventing you from accepting God's gift and experiencing the full power of the Holy Spirit in your life?

CLOSING THOUGHT

Dear God, no matter what I have heard or been taught, teach me to turn to you to understand what I do not understand. Lord — remind me that the Holy Spirit is a precious gift from you. Open my heart and mind as I challenge myself to make my relationship with you a daily journey.

Ducks and Geese and Wind — Oh My! (Part 2)

I was truly trying to explain the difference between wooden ducks and real ducks to Lukis. There are differences that seem easy to see, but from far away it may be more difficult. However, no matter how well crafted the wooden duck may be, the real duck has much more purpose and power to its life.

The same is true with our lives. We can choose to live a well crafted life without the power of the Holy Spirit and honestly, from far away — no one may notice — but you do. There is something inside of you that tugs at your heart and lingers in your mind because you know there is something more. In fact, you know exactly what God has called you to do — but instead you find safety in your wooden life.

Stop being safe! God has not only given you His son — He gave you the power of the Holy Spirit. He has never asked you to rely on your own power — He has offered you more – a divine power intended to fill you with purpose and help you be effective for Him. If this scares you, it absolutely should – you cannot do this on your own. The good news is, you don't have to!

"be strong – not in yourselves, but in the Lord, in the power of his boundless resource." Ephesians 6:20 (Phillips NT)

Think about it! Every Christ follower has the incredible, unbelievable opportunity to draw upon the divine power and wisdom of God himself to accomplish what He has purposefully created us to do. When we allow God to control us – to become intentional – to be led and empowered by the Holy Spirit – God begins to dwell in you – your thoughts, your mind, your heart, and your words. Who in the world would want to be a wooden duck?

Are you playing it safe? What is keeping you at a distance from what God has asked you to do with your life?

_____

_____

_____

_____

Who in the world would want to be a wooden duck?

CLOSING THOUGHT

God — teach me to no longer be safe — overwhelm me with your power. Lord, I pray that you overtake my mind, my thoughts, my heart and even my words. Let everything I do be with your power, and not my own.

Golf and Jesus

Lukis recently had quite a few discussions with his parents about God; about becoming a follower of Jesus. He had asked both Kelli and Levi as much as he could about the "logistics" of accepting Jesus into his heart.

It was evident that he definitely wanted Jesus to live there. So Lukis made a plan. He knew he was going to see Papa and hit golf balls. And when we were through, he would come back to Papa's house and that's when he would do it. He would ask Papa to pray with him and ask Jesus into his heart.

I was so amazed at his thought process and his incredible attention to detail not only asking about Jesus, but making sure that everything was just right, was amazing.

It reminded me of when we say, "I love you" for the first time, or prepare for the perfect marriage proposal. In that moment Lukis was making a decision to love Jesus and to live for Him. He truly wanted everything to be perfect – including hitting golf balls first.

Not only was I overjoyed, but I have to believe that it brought God so much joy that this precious child was so intentional and purposeful in how he would ask Jesus into his life. No – it doesn't take extravagance by any means, but what if we were that purposeful in our time we set aside for Him? Just like this devotional – are you looking forward to your time? Have you opened up your heart to hear what He has to say to you? Or are you rushing through it just so you can check it off your list? Let me encourage you – plan your time with Him – make it count. Pray before you start to read and pray after. Ask God to bring to your remembrance areas you need to work on – even if it's just setting aside time to fall in love with Him.

I love all who love me. Those who search will surely find me.
Proverbs 8:17 (NLT)

This is my commandment: Love each other in the same way I have loved you. John 15:12 (NLT)

When is the last time you told God you loved Him? Is there a special time you can plan just for Him?

In that moment Lukis was making a decision to love Jesus and to live for Him.

CLOSING THOUGHT

Lord – teach me to fall in love with you all over again. Remind me to set aside time just for you and me. I do love you, Lord – and I thank you for loving me.

Weekend Reflection

WEEK
4

What are my takeaways from this week?

_____

_____

What's true about me?

_____

_____

What do I want to be true about me?

_____

_____

How do I want to show up on Monday?

_____

_____

What needs to happen this weekend in order for this to be a reality?

_____

_____

WEEK

5

Living Forward

Are You Locked In?

Lukis loves the fact that I have a bathroom in my office. Truth be told, I like it too. One Sunday after service, Lukis asked if he could have the keys to my office. He said he needed to use the bathroom – actually, he needed to use my bathroom.

"I am waiting for you to rescue me because I can't get out!"

He took my keys and I continued talking with a few of our first-time guests. We had more visitors than usual that day, so I did not realize that Lukis had been gone a long time. His mom, Kelli, quickly walked up to me and said, "Lukis is locked in your office bathroom."

I remember he was quite upset. Apparently, he had been yelling for someone to help and Kelli heard him but could not open it from the outside. I felt terrible; I had failed to tell him not to lock the door. The lock was not working and needed to be repaired. I could only imagine the thought process Lukis must have gone through. The finality of being locked in this bathroom forever probably scared him. Lukis would miss our family lunch, and we were going to his favorite giant pancake place. It's one thing to be locked in a bathroom, but life without a giant pancake? Inconceivable! Obviously, panic set in.

By the time I made my way to the bathroom door, his mom had reassured him things would be ok. "Lukis what are you doing?" I asked. Through his tears, he said, "I am waiting for you to rescue me because I can't get out!" With a few instructions on how to jiggle the handle to pop the lock loose, he was out of the bathroom. For Lukis, that giant pancake was just a little bigger and better that day. Hugs felt better than ever, even from his sister. It had been a horrific experience and he felt grateful to be free.

Later, as I thought about Lukis' plight, I realized he could never have gotten out of that bathroom by himself. How do I know that? I have also been locked in that bathroom. Unless you know how to work the door knob (and sometimes that doesn't even work) you are stuck and need someone beyond yourself to be set free. Have you ever been stuck in life and been hesitant to ask for help? Yep, me too. A LOT! God says we can always call on Him and He'll set us free. Sometimes this happens in miraculous ways, or sometimes it takes place through someone who has the tools we need. It may not be in the way or the time we want, but help will come. You can count on it.

[56] *You listened when I called out, 'Don't shut your ears! Get me out of here! Save me!'* [57] *You came close when I called out. You said, 'It's going to be all right.'* Lamentations 3:56-57 (MSG)

[7] Listen, GOD, I'm calling at the top of my lungs: "Be good to me! Answer me!" [8] When my heart whispered, "Seek God," my whole being replied, "I'm seeking him!" Psalm 27:7-8 (MSG)

Do you feel stuck in a situation or area of your life? What is it?

_____

_____

_____

_____

CLOSING THOUGHT

Dear God – no matter how trapped I feel, remind me to call on you. Allow me to trust you with the rescue I need – in your time and in your way.

Running for your Life!

Lukis loves to remind his daddy how tall he is and how super fast he is as often as possible. It was probably through this confidence and casual conversation that Kelli (his mother) decided to sign up for the "fun run." This also meant a little running practice. After one mile, Lukis looked at his mother and said, "I wish we wouldn't have signed up for the fun run."

I agree Lukis – why run if you don't have to? I could not help but think of one Alabama and Auburn football game. Alabama led by five points with two minutes left and was twenty yards from the goal line. Their first-string quarterback was injured, which required the backup to step in. Alabama's Coach Bryant gave strict instructions to let the clock run down. On the fourth down, the quarterback went to hand off the ball, but he missed, forcing him to loft a pass. He did not see Auburn's safety, the fastest man on the field, just a few yards away. As soon as the ball was in the air, the Auburn safety cut in front of the Alabama receiver, pulled in the ball, and headed for the other end zone.

In a flash, the Alabama quarterback caught up with the swift safety. He tackled him on the two-yard line just as the clock ran out and Alabama won. After the game, Coach Bryant was asked, "I've read the scouting

Faith is running like your life depends on it.

reports. Your quarterback is supposed to be slow. How is it that he caught up with the fastest man on the field?" Bryant replied, "It's simple. Auburn was running for a touchdown. My man was running for his life!"

Maybe most of us only run when we have to – very similar to faith. We only use it when we have to – and even then we quickly give up. However, faith is running like your life depends on it. Faith is not letting your heart believe the situation is hopeless or the game is over.

God not only wants to bless you, He is looking for faithful people to bless. I think that's why God gave the illustration that it only takes the faith of a mustard seed to move the obstacle in your life. It doesn't take much faith; it just requires you to have it.

..."If you had faith even as small as a mustard seed, you could say to this mulberry tree be uprooted... and it would obey you." Luke 17:6 (NLT)

Refuse to let your heart believe the game is over and run for your life!

Have you convinced yourself that the game is over?

_____

_____

_____

_____

CLOSING THOUGHT

Lord – remind me of the small amount of faith you have asked me to have in you. Teach me to never allow my heart to believe in my circumstance, but instead have faith and run for my life!

What Do You See?

Lukis was almost six and was the youngest kid on his flag football team that summer. Although I chalk it up to talent, it may also help that his uncle is the coach.

We were so excited to see him play that our entire family on both sides showed up for his first football game. I'm not sure what I expected from his first game, but Lukis was more concerned that people kept pushing him and knocking him down.

After a few more games and lots of practice with his dad, he understood how the game was played. And this time, it was Lukis' turn to play quarterback. In the first play, he threw an incredible 15 yard spiral pass. I was so proud of his amazing pass – I didn't even care that it was intercepted. In fact, in my eyes, I saw the perfect pass.

As I reflected on my love for my grandson, my thoughts stumbled on this question: What if I saw that pass for exactly what it was – an interception? What if I was one of those parents or grandparents who began to immediately degrade his effort as a horrible mistake? Would Lukis continue to play, or would he begin to operate in a realm of fear?

In fact, in my eyes, I saw the perfect pass.

For many of you, your efforts were greeted with incredible criticism. You stopped trying just to prevent yourself from failing, never realizing that you were just one more try away from God's incredible purpose for your life. If you read nothing else, read this – even if you have quit, God has not given up on you!

Finish what you started in me, GOD. Your love is eternal—don't quit on me now. Psalm 138:8 (MSG)

Joe Montana, Hall of Fame Quarterback, led his team to four Super Bowls. Did you also know his first pass was an interception? Eventually, Lukis threw a touchdown pass. And by the time the season was complete, he loved playing football, loved his team and yes, I believe he's destined for the Hall of Fame – after all, that is what I see.

You may have lost sight of your purpose because someone or something has crushed your spirit or criticized your dream. You are afraid to try, and quite honestly you are not even sure how to move forward. Yet, you absolutely know and believe there is something more. I want to agree with you right now – God absolutely has a greater plan for your life than where you are today. It didn't matter to me that Lukis' first pass was intercepted, or even caught at all. I was just wrapped up in the perfect pass I saw – the same way God is wrapped up in how He sees you.

Are you convinced that God sees something perfect in you? What is holding you back?

God – remove the thoughts of criticism and fear of failure that have kept me from being the person you see. Give me the strength to try again – knowing you will always see the perfect me.

What's My Possible?

Troy Aikman was the number one overall draft pick in 1989. He finished his first season as a Dallas Cowboys quarterback with a 0-11 record. Not only that, Aikman threw twice as many interceptions as he did touchdowns.

He was determined to reach what was possible — His possible.

Instead of giving up, he went on to win more games than any other quarterback in the 1990s. Now he's in the Hall of Fame. He was determined to reach what was possible – His possible.

Everyone has dreams. Everyone has things to accomplish, but for some reason at some point in our lives we just get stuck. I wonder what would happen if we just stood back for a moment to remind ourselves of the dream we had in our heart. Think about the most common question we ask children — "What do you want to be when you grow up?" We love their answers, simply because at that moment in time — from astronaut to zoo keeper – anything is possible.

I have incredible thoughts and dreams for my grandson, Lukis. He absolutely loves all sports, so perhaps he will be an athlete. He has such a caring heart, so he could be a physician. He loves to wear a tie to church, so maybe he will be a pastor (our traditional service, of course). Truthfully, anything is possible for him, but what about us – what about you?

You are here - doing the farthest thing away from your heart's dream. I understand life happens and your heart's dream is just that — a dream. You may be in a situation where your financial commitments prevent you from doing anything else, or your education and talents are nowhere near what you think is needed to make this dream come to pass. You may have people in your life that would never support your dream, and rather than try or take the risk, it's much easier to live here – simply knowing there could be more.

"For God has not given us a spirit of fear and timidity, but of power, love, and self-discipline." 2 Timothy 1:7 (NLT)

I'm going to ask you to consider a few possibilities. What if the dream you have in your heart is too small? What if your finances are not even an issue for God? What if you absolutely have every ounce of education and talent God needs to make this dream come to pass? Will you trust him? What is possible for you? Remember these three key points: 1) Your possible is always connected to His purpose; 2) Your possible is always connected to God's people and the right people who support and help with feedback; and 3) Your possible always requires God's power (not yours).

Are you ready to discover your possible? What dreams are still vivid in your heart?

CLOSING THOUGHT

God – I pray that you remind me that I am on this earth for you. Teach me to make new decisions that will make the dream in my heart come to pass. Remind me to never limit you.

_____

_____

_____

_____

Happy Birthday Ol' Papa!

My grandson, Lukis, had called me on the phone to say happy birthday. He then asked two important questions: "Papa, how old are you?" I answered, "Fifty-four."

Without hesitation, he asked, "Are you going to have an ol' papa birthday party?" Wow – I guess I am an "ol' papa" – yet I couldn't help but smile.

Life really has happened so fast. I can remember as if it were yesterday when my son, Levi, was my grandson's age. That season in my life was unquestionably one of the most precious gifts and privileges in life, and yet I was young, inexperienced, and consequently missed savoring some of those special moments.

I have learned a few things as I've grown older. The early seasons of my life may not always have been within my control, but how I finish life is completely up to me. Lukis has a way of getting to the heart of the issue. He was right about this birthday; I would simply go home and spend a quiet evening with my wife. I truly was going to have an "ol' papa" birthday party. However, the evening would not be spent without reflecting on my life and thinking about the finish I want:

Finishing well continues to be my greatest focus these days.

Dave Beroth – Born: 1956 - Died: _____
He didn't miss life or mess it up.

CLOSING THOUGHT

Lord – let me finish this race well – with you. I pray that I use every gift you have given me, every talent I have to share and every moment of time with the people you have given me to love.

I wouldn't mind if the above epitaph is what my grandson reflects upon at my grave side. It would mean I finished well. It would mean that I practiced the title and essence of Eugene Peterson's book, *A Long Obedience in the Same Direction.*

6 As for me, my life has already been poured out as an offering to God. The time of my death is near. 7 I have fought the good fight, I have finished the race, and I have remained faithful. 2 Timothy 4:6-7 (NLT)

Finishing well continues to be my greatest focus these days. Finishing well is not easy and it does not mean finishing unblemished or finishing perfect. Rather, it is finishing as one who overcomes personal failures and life's setbacks by embracing the grace of God.

No matter how your life has started – have you thought about what it means to finish well? How do you want to be remembered?

_____

_____

_____

_____

Weekend Reflection

What are my takeaways from this week?

_____

_____

What's true about me?

_____

_____

What do I want to be true about me?

_____

_____

How do I want to show up on Monday?

_____

_____

What needs to happen this weekend in order for this to be a reality?

_____

_____

WEEK

5

My Life Forward Coaching

Every day, we make choices to do or not do many things. These choices may range from profound to trivial. Each one has an effect that makes our lives more fulfilling or less fulfilling, more balanced or less balanced, more effective or less effective.

Life coaching helps you learn how to make choices that create an effective, balanced and fulfilling life.

Life Coaching is profoundly different from consulting, mentoring, giving advice, getting therapy, or seeking counseling. It is action-oriented, solution-oriented, and concentrates on forward motion, not looking at the past.

The coaching process addresses your specific personal projects, business successes, and conditions and transitions in your personal life, relationships or profession through the lens of what is going on right now. Discover your obstacles or challenges, and choose a course of action to make your life be what you want it to be.

Dave is passionate about seeing you successfully navigate challenges in the heat of leadership and ministry so you find joy and fulfillment in your calling. Through powerful, engaging one-on-one

MYLIFEFORWARD.COM

Visit *mylifefoward*.com to read Dave's encouraging blogs and request your complimentary coaching session.

coaching sessions, Dave helps highly motivated church and business leaders discover their full contribution and solidify their passion.

Discover and practice healthy thought patterns, develop behavioral habits that lead to strong relationships and a healthy marriage and family life, and gain credibility and work successfully with the right opportunities that are available.

Notes